KEEP MOVING

ALLOWING GOD TO FULFILL VISION THROUGH YOU

BISHOP RUTH SMITH HOLMES

MORE EXCELLENT
WAY ENTERPRISES

Scripture references are taken from the King James Version
of the Holy Bible unless otherwise noted.
Pronouns for referring to the Father, Son and Holy Spirit are
capitalized intentionally and the words devil and satan is
never capitalized.

Publisher:
MEWE, LLC
Lithonia, GA
www.mewellc.com

First Edition
ISBN: 978-0-692-29116-0

For Worldwide Distribution
Printed in the USA

Dedication

This book is dedicated to my mother, Lee Ethel
Williams; my loving husband, Dr. Rickie Holmes;
and all the Smith Holmes children, God-children
and spiritual children as well as ALL the people
who want to Keep Moving!

Acknowledgement

I would like to thank and acknowledge the
Late Archbishop Jimmie Lee Smith, founder and
mentor of Light of the World Christian Tabernacle
International, who answered the call of God to share
the gospel of Jesus Christ around the world and
equipped others to do the same.

Table of Content

Foreword

Bishop Ruth Smith Holmes is a very compassionate leader who is full of great insight. In her latest book, *Keep Moving*, Bishop Ruth reveals many life changing tools in the confounds of each chapter. From the beginning until the end, great information will jump out at you. Knowing God's purpose for humanity is a must especially for those who are laboring in this vineyard called life.

Oftentimes, we look at Adam and Eve and their fall without looking at their God-given responsibilities. God gave Adam commands that he needed to complete. God did not expect Adam to do nothing; instead, he expected Adam to keep moving forward to carry out the commands.

The revelation of who you are is very important in order to keep moving. As I explore my own life through this prolific writing of Bishop Ruth, I can't help but feel the need to keep moving in spite of tests, trials, and tribulations.

I learned at a very young age that certain information is very valuable for success. We serve a God of information, details, and principles. As you read this book, let it soak into the fiber of your soul and I guarantee you that you will *Keep Moving*.

- Dr. Robbi Warren
Television Evangelist & Author

Preface

It is essential to understand how our moving and serving in the kingdom of God can have a lasting and positive effect on not only our own lives, but also on the lives of others. God created mankind to do something. In the Garden of Eden, He instructed Adam to name the animals, to exercise dominion, and to be fruitful and multiply.

And God blessed them, and God said unto them, Be fruitful, and multiply, and replenish the earth, and subdue it: and have dominion over the fish of the sea, and over the fowl of the air, and over every living thing that moveth upon the earth. (Genesis 1:28)

And out of the ground the Lord God formed every beast of the field, and every fowl of the air; and brought them unto Adam to see what he would call them: and whatsoever Adam called every living creature, that was the name thereof. (Genesis 2:19)

To carry out God's commands, Adam had to do something. So, from the beginning, God's plan was for mankind to do something – to keep moving. We cannot stop; we must continue to move forward.

Go and Teach All Nations

God didn't stop giving commands and expecting His people to do something after Adam left the Garden of Eden; He, even today, expects His people to be obedient to the commands found in His Word. As Christians, our primary duty is to carry out the Great Commission:

> *Go ye therefore, and teach all nations, baptizing them in the name of the Father, and of the Son, and of the Holy Ghost: Teaching them to observe all things whatsoever I have commanded you: and, lo, I am with you always, even unto the end of the world. Amen.* (Matthew 28:19–20)

Jesus said that we must GO and that we must TEACH the gospel everywhere. Why is it important that we go and teach in all nations? The world is filled with hurting people. Hurting people who are saved and need Jesus to heal them and hurting people who are lost and need Jesus to save them. Jesus Christ is the answer. He is the hope of the world; He is the "hope of glory" (see Colossians 1:27).

Christ needs you to be the vehicle He uses to show love in the world. We must be willing to do what God commands through the Word and also by the leading of the Holy Spirit. In other words, we must be willing to do something to help fulfill the vision that God places in our hearts to bring hope to the world.

Over the years I have heard many people say, "I am waiting on the Lord," for one reason or another. Well, I am here to tell you that God is waiting on us—He is waiting on us to do something—something that will change our lives and the lives of those around us—our family, our community, our world.

Activate the Power Within

Our doing something activates the power within us to move on our behalf. Imagine having the key to access a room, but not putting the key in the lock to open the door. Putting the key in the lock and turning it is the do something that is needed to open the door. Having a key in your hand is great, but it is not enough to access your potential…your promise…your purpose. Turn the key—do something—to gain access. In the same way, a car can't go forward—I don't care if the gas tank is full—if no one gets in the car and turns it on and presses the pedal. You have to do something in order for the car to function in the purpose for which it was created—to move.

Beyond Hearing and Receiving

The Bible says in Mark 4:20, "And these are they which are sown on good ground; such as hear the word, and receive it, and bring forth fruit, some thirtyfold, some sixty, and some an hundred." To "bring forth fruit," one must do something. Furthermore, this Scripture indicates that our level of obedience in doing something correlates to how much we will reap for our actions. There has to be work…there has to be action…there has to be something beyond hearing and receiving—that something is *doing*.

The bible lets us know that it is important to do the Word and not just hear the Word, *"But be ye doers of the word, and not hearers only, deceiving your own selves."* (James 1:22) Hearing the Word and even having faith in the Word is not enough. Our faith must be demonstrated by action.

Even so faith, if it hath not works, is dead, being alone. Yea, a man may say, Thou hast faith, and I have works: shew me thy faith without thy works, and I will shew thee my faith by my works. Thou believest that there is one God; thou doest well: the devils also believe, and tremble. But wilt thou know, O vain man, that faith without works is dead? (James 2:17–20)

It's Time for Greater Works

Jesus, as He walked this earth, was our greatest example of doing something. He healed, He comforted, He prayed, He taught, He loved, He helped, He fed, He gave…He did something. He told His disciples in John 14:12, "Verily, verily, I say unto you, He that believeth on me, the works that I do shall he do also; and greater works than these shall he do; because I go unto my Father."

Do you believe on the Lord Jesus Christ? Then it is time for you to allow Him to guide you to greater works. Now is not the time to stop. Keep moving!

- Bishop Ruth W. Smith Holmes

Chapter 1

Healed to Help

Our lives, churches, and businesses are filled with hurting and broken people and the enemy wants to destroy the very people that Jesus came and died for. No matter what transgression a person has committed, Jesus died for that person and if he or she were important enough for the Son of God to give His life, then they should be important enough for us to seek them—to help them. Since Jesus gave His life for all of us, we should be grateful for His sacrifice by doing what He did and more. *"Verily, verily, I say unto you, he that believeth on me, the works that I do shall he do also; and greater works than these shall he do; because I go unto my Father."* (John 14:12)

Our lives, churches, and businesses are also filled with people whom God has already equipped to do something about the brokenness and hopelessness that this world experiences. You have already been equipped and called to keep moving and it must be done now!

If we're going to keep moving, we must allow God to do something in us first and foremost. Before we can help the broken, we must have our brokenness mended as well. Many of us are broken and trying to help others, and because we are also broken, we actually end up creating more issues and problems than we are helping to mend. It is important for us to learn about being equipped to make the difference that God says we can make and that we should make.

As you exercise your faith and empower people, use these words to empower you to keep moving. Sometimes, when we are talking to people, they are very distraught about their condition and all we need to do is listen and say to them, "Keep moving" and that will activate their faith. It will also motivate them to take appropriate actions, according to the Word, to help themselves.

I declare that it is time to release you to go beyond your fears, anxieties, inhibitions, and everything that might hold you up. It is time to release you to do something for the Kingdom of God. One of the most powerful things that I find to be true is when we work for God, God works for us!

An important question to ask yourself is what is it that you need God to do in you that you might be free to help the next person? What do you need Him to strengthen in you? Do you need boldness? Do you need courage or vision or compassion? What is it that you need? For me, God said He wanted to take me out of my comfort zone. He said that I am quite accomplished in the circle that I am currently in, but He wants to take me in a circle to do things that I have not already done and to go places where I have never been. This is not a very comfortable place for me. However, He said, "In order for me to lead you further, you have to go further." God said also, "There's no other way for Me to take you where you have never been until you come out of your comfort zone." Therefore, my spiritual journey has literally just begun. So, I made a commitment to God to come out of my comfort zone, and if I am going to reach for greater heights for the Kingdom, I must do it. I believe that God Himself will meet me at this new stage in every turn that I make, every move I make; and He will hear every prayer for strength and success.

Remember, God has called us and anointed us for this season. We need to embrace and heed that call. We are the light of the world. Jesus said in John 8:12, "*I am the light of the world,*" and as the Church, the body of Christ, we are the light of the world, so we have the name to live up to. We are to be the light in the world and we are required to go and to do as purposes for our lives. Aren't you glad that God decided to use you? What a privilege that God will make a decision to use you and me—just ordinary people—to do extraordinary things.

Oftentimes, we look at people who are well accomplished and we think they are exceptional people. They are merely exceptional because they've done something beyond the ordinary. You can be exceptional, too, and you can do great work in the Kingdom!

Do not allow anything to come against your efforts to keep moving in God or to give you the notion that you are unable to act or achieve great things. Let's take a look at the things that come against us.

Lack of Trust

Many times we value what God does based upon what people have done. If you don't remember anything else, remember to not compare God to people. Don't measure Him against mommy, daddy, sister, cousin, pastor, or anyone else that you know. God is not like man. He's somebody above all that we can imagine or think, and He says His ways are not our ways and His thoughts are not our thoughts. (See Isaiah 55:8) So don't measure God based upon this tangible world. If you measure Him based on this tangible world, you will always be disappointed because you will look at Him and judge Him and think He's going to behave like man behaves. Remember, God is faithful and He's faithful all the time.

Lack of Accountability

Most people do not like accountability. We like to do our own thing, so if we want to do our own thing, we get a little nervous when somebody says you need to do something a certain way. But accountability is extremely important in Kingdom work. Proverbs 27:17 says, *"Iron sharpeneth iron; so a man sharpeneth the countenance of his friend."* Accountability is important, but we push back against it because we it keeps us from doing what we want. Thus, we are more likely to ignore God and we are less likely to submit to Him if we are not being held accountable. When we are not held accountable, we will attempt to deny God, and we will not submit to what He says.

Lack of Confidence

I have spent too much time trying to figure out if God really knows what He's doing, especially when it has to do with my life. Do you have the confidence to believe God really knows what's best for you? When trials and trouble start to rise up, sometimes God is giving you a word, a hint, or a wise warning. He's telling you what He wants you to do. Then, you begin to ask yourself, "Was it really God? "Is it God?" "Did God say it?" and then you say, "Well, if God's telling me to do something and it's going to be like this, I don't recognize nor do I desire to follow what God is saying to me."

I know there are some things that God says to me and I say, "Lord, really? For real?" This is a case where we lack the confidence that God's plan is really best for us.

We do not like how God wants it done. We do not like the order and message from Him. We do not like the fact that what He says may bring a little embarrassment and shame to our situation.

Sometimes, we have so much pride and dignity to the point that God can't even use us. But I tell you, if you mess around and say "Yes" to God, you will be amazed at what He will do with your situation.

It is impossible to have confidence in a God that we do not trust, so we have to learn to trust Him no matter what. Furthermore, it is difficult to have confidence in a God we can't see, mainly because we like tangible things. I like tangible things as much or more than anybody, but I have learned that I must trust and follow God, whom I cannot see in the natural, but I have confidence in Him through His Word.

Lack of Nurturing

We go through this journey of life with its myriad of challenges and sometimes we do not sense that God is right there with us. He seems so far away sometimes. But He is not far away; He is right there with us all the time. When you don't feel Him, you need to believe He is there. God is right here—carrying, nurturing, and protecting you.

Philippians 1:6 tells us, *"He which hath begun a good work in you will perform it until the day of Jesus Christ."* He is saying that He is never going to leave you and He will be with you until Jesus comes back for you. That's good news to me and to all of us. Just pause for a moment and reflect on His promise that He will work on us until Jesus comes back for us. So, we don't have to fret and think that God is going to disappear. God is not going anywhere. He will work on us until Jesus returns for us. He is always working on our behalf in order to complete the work of the Kingdom.

Chapter 2

Moving in Purpose

There is a simple principle behind everything we do. We must know the purpose. There's a saying: If we do not know the purpose of a thing, we will abuse it. Knowing our purpose will help us understand, not only as individuals, but also collectively, the importance of fulfilling our life's eternal goals. Matthew 22:37-40 says:

> *Jesus said unto him, Thou shalt love the Lord thy God with all thy heart, and with all thy soul, and with all they mind. This is the first and great commandment. And the second is like unto it, Thou shall love thy neighbour as thyself. On these two commandments hang all the law and the prophets.*

We must also understand we have life's eternal goals and purposes beyond what we see right now and part of fulfilling our purpose is to help others fulfill their purpose.

Our Primary Purpose

Our primary purpose is to love God with all our hearts. We were created to love God and if we love God, then we will love those around us and ourselves. The two-million-dollar question is: How do we love God? Oftentimes, we are told we should do something, but the fact is, we don't know how to do what needs to be done. How do we love God with all our hearts?

What Is Love?

The first thing we must do is understand God's perspective. According to Matthew 22:38, love is described as, *"This is the first and great commandment."* This is exactly what Jesus did, and He understood His purpose. Not only did Jesus say this was our number one commandment, He also understood as well as demonstrated that it was His number one commandment.

The life of Jesus is an example of the perfect love of God. As we deal with the perfect love of God, we must understand that Jesus exemplified who God was while on earth. He showed us how to love our enemies by loving His enemies. Jesus did exactly what He told us to do. He showed us how to love by exemplifying it in front of His disciples as well as those who lived in that day and time. Jesus' very life was used to demonstrate God's perfect love toward us. When we see Jesus, we see the Father. In spite of the fact that we don't see Him in the natural, we see Him by the Word. Those who saw Him in the natural do not have any more on us because John 20:29 tells us, *"Jesus saith unto him, Thomas, because thou hast seen me, thou hast believed: blessed are they that have not seen, and yet have believed."*

It is critical to know our purpose in life and know how to accomplish our purpose. How are we supposed to get where we are going? We need a map or GPS. It is important that we have the Holy Spirit because when we are confused about what the Holy Spirit is saying to us, we can pull out the Bible and receive specific directions regarding where we should go. Direction eliminates confusion about what the Holy Spirit is saying to us. If we are not sure, we need to pick up our Bible to check it out in the Scripture. We need to know where we're going on the journey.

God has a very clear and simple purpose behind everything He has for us to do. It's really simple. Love! We are called to love God, our friends, and ourselves. He also said we must love our enemies. That's why we have to keep the Bible in front of us. When it really comes down to our enemies, we are a little slower to love them than we might be with our friends. God wants us to love our enemies as much as we love our friends.

Because I was challenged to express love, the most revolutionary event in my life occurred when God didn't expect me, in my natural self, to show love. Although I felt loved, I was challenged to really show it. I was straightforward in my approach to others, and it didn't always feel like love when I was talking. However, God said to me,

"No one is really loving in and of themselves." He further explained that people with pleasant personalities are not any more loving than me. The only way one can really show love is through God. When we love people, it is not us loving them; instead, it is God working through us to love them. Even the person with the most stubborn spirit can love people. It is God loving through them and not them trying to muster up love.

Obedience Is Key

How do we love one may ask? Do we say nice things and/or do we feel good about things? Are the aforementioned questions the keys to love? No, love is simply obedience! When we love God, we obey God. We can say, "I love You, Lord," nevertheless, if we present contradicting behavior, then we really don't love God. Many people brag and celebrate loving the Lord despite the fact that when we look at their lifestyle, it is not in alignment with loving the Lord. In order to love God we must obey Him."

The underlying purpose of our life is to do something in obedience to God. It's not enough just to talk about it; we must do something. If God tells us to scoop, sit, or stand, then we should just do it. We don't have to understand it all, but we have to be obedient. This journey of life must be one of continuous acts of obedience. Once we obey God in one thing, then there's something else that we must obey Him in. That's why we really don't arrive in this life—we are always moving in a progression of obedience, and disobedience costs us so much. Disobedience gets us off course, and then there's a price to be paid in that disobedience. In addition, there is recovery that has to happen and it's very costly. It's really not worth it! The price we pay is just too much to invest. If we make it our business to obey God with everything, He says to us—it's not how much money we have, it's not how many friends we have, it's not even how many people we help, because if God did not say help them, it is still disobedience.

I see people all the time who are in excess in helping and some of them destitute themselves trying to help and really don't have themselves stabilized. I ask the question, "Why are you worried about Mary when you have a household that needs your attention. Why are you across the street? Go home and take care of your household." We have to remember that it's not about whether we're doing something, it's about if we're doing what God said to do. Obedience is the primary example of how we show our love to God.

Understand that God knows what we should do because many times as we reach out to people, *not that we shouldn't help people*, we abort the opportunity to trust God. We abort their opportunity to grow in God, and then we abort our opportunity because we're being disobedient. Therefore, you ought to be very prayerful and you should hear the voice of God as do for others.

We prove we love God when we obey Him, and when we obey Him, we do just what He says, and we only do that which He has prepared us to do. We never have to worry about trying to do something that God hasn't prepared us to do; He always prepares us to do that which He tells us to do. Our job is to be obedient because He has prepared us. To live this life of obedience, we must make sure that Jesus is on the throne of our hearts. It's not about us; it's all about Him and what He says.

Philippians 2:5-10 speaks about how even Christ on the cross learned obedience:

> *Let this mind be in you, which was also in Christ Jesus: Who, being in the form of God, thought it not robbery to be equal with God: But made himself of no reputation, and took upon him the form of a servant, and was made in the likeness of men: And being found in fashion as a man, he humbled himself, and became obedient unto death, even the death of the cross. Wherefore God also hath highly exalted him, and given him a name which is above every name: That at the name of Jesus every knee should bow, of things in heaven, and things in earth, and things under the earth.*

It was an act of obedience for Him to die on the cross. He could have said "No" and this world would still been in sin. But He chose to obey God. Aren't you glad? Sometimes, we think about Jesus in terms of, *He was Jesus so He had to come and He had to do.* No! He made choices just like we do. He just chose to be obedient to the Father. Are you making a choice to be obedient to the Father? I made a choice to push forward and strive to be more obedient to what God is telling me.

Romans 5:19 tells us, *"For as by one man's disobedience many were made sinners, so by the obedience of one shall many be made righteous."* Many will be made righteous through Jesus' obedience. Without His obedience, we wouldn't need to be righteous. As we are obedient, we also win others to Christ. It's not just about us. When we're obedient, others see our example and can follow us. As Paul said, *"Be ye followers of me, even as I also am of Christ."* (1 Corinthians 11:1) Why? Because I'm going to be obedient to what He has said for me to do.

Hebrews 5:8 says, *"Though he were a Son, yet learned he obedience by the things which he suffered."* Jesus' suffering was an act of obedience. Many of us will be challenged with several difficult situations this year. Some of them won't feel so good, but I promise you, in Christ, that the difficulties are working for your good. I also promise that if you stay obedient, even through the challenging times, your obedience and suffering will also exemplify your love for God. Instead of complaining, you will love God and inspire others to be faithful in spite of the circumstances in their lives. They will, in turn, learn how to suffer and yet stay in Christ.

When I suffered in the past, I complained and whined a lot, but I have made up my mind to just give God praise all day…to praise Him no matter what I'm feeling…no matter what the thought is, just give God praise to show my love for Him! That's a good opportunity to show the love I have for God.

The more you press, the more you praise God or show your love for Him. The enemy expects you to act a certain way when you are pressed, but because you love God and you love yourself, your neighbors, and your enemies, it really doesn't matter what people are doing or not doing because you are here to give God the glory in spite of it all.

It is amazing how powerful we are—not in ourselves, but God in us. It's the hope of glory! Once in a while, you will hear people say, "You don't know my story so you don't understand my glory," but we can see it. We can see the glory of God on a life that is obedient to God. It doesn't matter what we have on or don't have on.

Obedience has to be based on the Word of God. Love has to be based upon the Word of God.

Some love relationships don't look like the love that I know according to the Word of God. We have to make sure that we are living according to truth. We cannot make the Word say what we want it to say, and we cannot fix the Word so it fits our situation. Whatever God has said, it is right.

Can you think about your life, places you have been and choices you have made over time and then look at yourself today and realize that since you moved from that place, you have made progress and have actually gotten some things right with God? I thank God for the things that I've gotten right with Him. I thank God for the mind to continue to get things right with Him. I also thank God I don't have the mindset that "I have arrived."

It doesn't matter how close we think we are to God. It doesn't matter how many tongues we talk in or how much anointing is on our life. Let me tell you, we have not arrived—not as long as we are in this flesh. Before you know it, unintended thoughts seep in your mind and although your mind should be focusing on Jesus, other thoughts avail themselves.

We have not arrived; however, God is with us, and we have to base our love on truth, righteousness, and holiness.

Jesus told His disciples He would send the Holy Spirit to be our helper and He would lead us into all truth.

John 16:13 states:

Howbeit when he, the Spirit of truth, is come, he will guide you into all truth: for he shall not speak of himself; but whatsoever he shall hear, that shall he speak: and he will shew you things to come.

The Holy Spirit is in you, and He is here to lead us into all truth and to help us in our weakness and infirmities that we might not just know we are weak, but that we might do better. We're talking about the love of God and obedience to God. That's our main responsibility.

Think for just a moment about some area of your life when you were struggling or when you were out of the will of God. You have gotten it right. That should make you rejoice and give thanks! Now think about an area of your life that is not quite on point yet. Do you know how you're going to get there? The same way you got the other situations resolved. You have to do something to make the shift.

Respond to Challenges with the Word

Jesus was frequently confronted with leaders who thought they could outsmart Him. Of course, they could not. I think that every generation thinks it can outsmart God and will try from time to time because they think they know a little bit more about their situation than God does. Even when we pray and He explains how to answer our prayers exactly, there are still those of us who think we can outsmart or out think Him. Well, I am here to tell you that God really does know what He's doing.

In John Chapter 8, Jesus was challenged on His teaching regarding adultery. In verses 6-9, He gives an answer to that particular challenge that states:

> *This they said, tempting him, that they might have to accuse him. But Jesus stooped down, and with his finger wrote on the ground, as though he heard them not. So when they continued asking him, he lifted up himself, and said unto them, He that is without sin among you, let him first cast a stone at her. And again he stooped down, and wrote on the ground. And they which heard it, being convicted by their own conscience, went out one by one, beginning at the eldest, even unto the last: and Jesus was left alone, and the woman standing in the midst.*

Whenever Jesus was challenged, He responded with the Word. That helps us realize that, "Okay," He's seeing beyond where we are thinking. Too much discussion is made about being right. We are the light of the world and our response to situations should be what the Word says.

Jesus gave us another point in John 8:14 that states, *"Jesus ans wered and said unto them,*

*Though I bear record of myself, yet my record is true: for I know whence I came, and whither I go; but ye cannot tell whence I come, and whither I go.***"** He was talking to His disciples about leaving them and their not being able to come with Him. He explained to them the light of the world by talking about knowing where He was going and from where He came. He wanted them to know there was no darkness in Him.

Jesus talked about unbelief in John 8:28. *"Then said Jesus unto them, When ye have lifted up the Son of man, then shall ye know that I am he, and that I do nothing of myself; but as my Father hath taught me, I speak these things."*

Jesus gave several accounts in Matthew 19:16-24, including, but limited to, talking to a rich young ruler who thought he could outsmart Jesus with questions about how to get to heaven.

And, behold, one came and said unto him, Good Master, what good thing shall I do, that I may have eternal life? And he said unto him, Why callest thou me good? there is none good but one, that is, God: but if thou wilt enter into life, keep the commandments. He saith unto him, Which? Jesus said, Thou shalt do no murder, Thou shalt not commit adultery, Thou shalt not steal, Thou shalt not bear false witness, Honour thy father and thy mother: and, Thou shalt love thy neighbour as thyself. The young man saith unto him, All these things have I kept from my youth up: what lack I yet? Jesus said unto him, If thou wilt be perfect, go and sell that thou hast, and give to the poor, and thou shalt have treasure in heaven: and come and follow me. But when the young man heard that saying, he went away sorrowful: for he had great possessions. Then said Jesus unto his disciples, Verily I say unto you, That a rich man shall hardly enter into the kingdom of heaven. And again I say unto you, It is easier for a camel to go through the eye of a needle, than for a rich man to enter into the kingdom of God.

Jesus helped the rich young ruler and the disciples understand one cannot get to heaven by good works. A person must be born again! Jesus cannot and will not be outsmarted by anyone. He is omniscient; therefore, He knows everything. He knows our purpose and we must move in our purpose regardless of our social or financial status – obedience to God is the way.

Chapter 3

Before Moving Forward

As recorded in Matthew 4:1-11, Jesus was tempted on the official first day of His ministry. He was baptized in the River Jordan by John and immediately went into the wilderness for forty days to fast and pray. There He was confronted by satan. In this story, we learn that Jesus was completely prepared to deal with satan on the first day. The lesson for us is that we must also fast and pray. Sometimes, we don't think we're prepared, because the enemy has slipped one in on us; but know that we—and you--are completely prepared to deal with the devil.

It is critical that we are aware of and confident that God has made every preparation necessary for us to be successful in this journey. When I say successful, I mean that we are able to do everything that God has assigned us to do. You don't have to worry about what God didn't assign to you. All you have to focus on is what God told you to do. Furthermore, learn from everybody around you, but don't become the average *anybody*. Because the best person you can be is you! I think—a lot of times—about how people do what they do, but every time I think about it, I hear God saying, "Be you, do you!"

Remember, Jesus said, *"Verily, verily, I say unto you, He that believeth on me, the works that I do shall he do also; and greater works than these shall he do; because I go unto my Father"* (John 14:12). Isn't that unimaginable when you think about what Jesus did? But we really should be doing more than He did, and we can. It's not complicated. If there is something going on in a person's life, it doesn't necessarily require us to pray forever. It simply requires us to speak to the situation and spiritually speak into existence a new and confident path to follow.

It is not necessary to hang around to see that the problem is gone or see what happened. All we have to do is speak to the situation and go on to the next opportunity with confidence. We spend a lot of time laboring with stuff that we really don't need to be concerned with, and this wastes time and keeps us from doing other valuable work that we should be doing.

Tools and Weapons

In this process of doing God's work, we can be assured that God will give us tools and weapons to successfully complete the tasks. Tools are used to do a work. Weapons are used to fight. You need both of them in this walk with God. Keep in mind you will have to fight for some things to happen and you will have to build other things to succeed. Jesus would never challenge us to do something He hasn't equipped us to do. First Corinthians 10:13 tells us,

There hath no temptation taken you but such as is common to man: but God is faithful, who will not suffer you to be tempted above that ye are able; but will with the temptation also make a way to escape, that ye may be able to bear it.

Therefore, we will never be tempted or burdened with anything God has not prepared us to handle. Jesus was never at a loss for words, for power, for answers to any questions He faced when He was tempted. Whether is required mental acuity or physical stamina to complete His job, God was always within Him. You can be assured that He will be there for you, too!

We're Jesus people! As a Jesus person, you have all the grace on your life that Jesus had on His life as He walked this Earth. He didn't work in the earth as a god; He worked in the earth as a man. He's our example. We have the same grace on our lives. He relied on the preparation, wisdom, and faith He knew He had received from God the Father.

Our Tools: The Holy Spirit

Understand this: The main thing Jesus had working for Him was the Holy Spirit. We have that same need—to be filled with the Holy Spirit. If you're not filled with the Holy Spirit, you are trying to do the work on your own and failure is inevitable. Again, you must have the Holy Spirit. The Holy Spirit has a work for us, and we are in trouble if we try to accomplish work in our lives without Him. We can't be saved in Jesus and not have the Holy Spirit. Moreover, we do not have the power that it takes to do something without the Holy Spirit.

Jesus told His disciples, *"But when the Comforter is come, whom I will send unto you from the Father, even the Spirit of truth, which proceedeth from the Father, he shall testify of me"* (John 15:26). The Holy Spirit testified of Jesus, so when we have the Holy Spirit, we must also testify of Jesus!

Jesus said, *"And when he is come, he will reprove the world of sin, and of righteousness, and of judgment"* (John 16:8). In other words, He will convict us of sin. So, when we have the Holy Spirit, we are also convicted of sin.

Jesus said that the Holy Spirit, *"will guide you into all truth: for he shall not speak of himself; but whatsoever he shall hear, that shall he speak: and he will shew you things to come, will lead us into all truth"* (John 16:13). We have the Holy Spirit and we know the truth will stand forever.

Romans 8:26 says, *"The Spirit also helpeth our infirmities: for we know not what we should pray for as we ought: but the Spirit itself maketh intercession for us with groanings which cannot be uttered.*" The Holy Spirit helps us when we pray. Do we need help in prayer? Yes we do! Prayer changes things. Prayer is our best tool. Jesus said, *Ye shall receive power, after that the Holy Spirit is come upon you: and ye shall be witnesses unto me both in Jerusalem, and in all Judaea, and in Samaria, and unto the uttermost part of the earth.* (Acts 1:8)

In order to serve God, we must be filled with the Holy Spirit, who gives us power. Part of our successful preparation for work is the Holy Spirit's being in us. Romans 8:11 tells us: "*If the Spirit of him that raised up Jesus from the dead dwell in you, he that raised up Christ from the dead shall also quicken your mortal bodies by his Spirit that dwelleth in you.*"

The Holy Spirit will raise us up from the dead. So when we're praying for the sick, the afflicted, the spiritually dead and those who are almost at the point of physical death, we believe God to raise them up. It is the Holy Spirit who will quicken their mortal flesh and raise them up again! When we're ministering to people, we need to understand that the work of the Holy Spirit is not our job. All we have to do is activate the power within us by the Holy Spirit. We speak life and God does the rest.

Ephesians 3:16 says, "*Take unto you the whole armour of God, that ye may be able to withstand in the evil day, and having done all, to stand.*" The Holy Spirit will strengthen us and give us strength for this journey. There are times when we have been out all day long and then we have to be someplace else; but every time we make a stop, it's like something happens—there's a refreshing. I take care of that assignment and then I get in the car and say, "Whooo, can we go home now?"

Sometimes at the end of the day I am reminded that I have one more stop I need to make because I promised someone we would visit. By the time I get there, a surge of energy comes, and the anointing comes up on me and I do what I need to do. I say all of that to tell you that God always refreshes me for the work that I need to do. Have you ever experienced God's refreshing? You know you should be exhausted and to the point of quitting, but the Lord keeps nudging and saying, "You can go on; if you say yes to Me, I will hold you up one more day, one more hour, one more minute. I will refresh you and cause it to be so."

Our Tools: The Bible

The second tool that God gives us is the Bible—the Word of God. The best thing you and I have going for us is the Word. Whatever comes before you, the Word is your answer. Don't ever forget that the Word is your resource—not the counselor or therapist, but the Word. If you get the Word in you, it will make a difference. God prepared the Old Testament for Jesus to use.

28

If you read Matthew 4:4, you will learn that Jesus was tempted by the devil, but He answered and said, "*It is written: 'Man shall not live by bread alone, but by every word that proceedeth out of the mouth of God.*" It was the Word that helped Jesus to receive victory over the enemy. He didn't cuss, fuss, swear, fall out or do any of that. He simply said, "It is written!" He understood the power in the Word of God. We know that God's Word is the basis and the answer for everything.

Jesus would say all the time, "It is written" in the laws and the prophecy. We should also be saying, "It is written" in the Word of God. If you say what the Word says, you can receive victory after victory! So many times, that's all God is asking us to do—to stand in the gap with faith for someone until he can rise up and testify for himself.

Sometimes, we don't want to confess the Word over a person who is sick, just in case the person doesn't make it. That is the devil speaking to us, and he is a liar! Speak the Word! The Bible says the Lord watches over his Word to perform it. Jeremiah 1:12 states, "*Then said the Lord unto me, Thou hast well seen: for I will hasten my word to perform it.*" We're giving up too many victories by setting ourselves in agreement with what the devil is saying. Make a decision that you are not going to set yourself in agreement with the devil on anything. Speak the Word. Believe God for the impossible. If we can do a thing, we do not need God in it. But the things God is telling us to do, we cannot do without Him. This is the year of double blessings, but I'm telling you, we are going to have to work for those victories!

The Holy Spirit will lead us into all truth. Everything we need to know, the Holy Spirit will make know to us. Jesus quoted the Bible in every tempting situation. When He talked about murdering, He said, *"Rejoice, and be exceeding glad: for great is your reward in heaven: for so persecuted they the prophets which were before you"* (Matthew 5:12).

When He dealt with adultery, He said, *"Ye have heard that it was said by them of old time, Thou shalt not commit adultery"* (Matthew 5:27). When He talked about taking an oath, He said, *"Again, ye have heard that it hath been said by them of old time, Thou shalt not forswear thyself, but shalt perform unto the Lord thine oaths"* (Matthew 5:33). When He talked about love, He said, *"Therefore all things whatsoever ye would that men should do to you, do ye even so to them: for this is the law and the prophets"* (Matthew 7:12). He spoke the Word, relied on the Word and believed in the Word.

We don't have to argue with people about what they are doing. Just speak the Word! When you know the Word, you don't have to get into an argument. You know what the Word says, don't you? After you tell people what the Word says, you just go on. Simply give them this life-saving message and allow the Holy Spirit to do the fighting. There is no reason to pick a fight. Give them the Word and keep it moving.

Our Tools: Prayer

God prepared us with prayer as a means of communicating with Him. The gospel writer Luke states that Jesus withdrew into the wilderness and prayed. (Luke 5:16) And if He had to pray, we certainly need to pray. This is the season for us to stop talking about prayer and begin praying! There's an opportunity for powerful and real prayer time. I have been quite amazed that more people are not interested in praying. The prayers that we verbalize on Sunday mornings are just introductory prayers, but I'm talking about really spending time at the altar on behalf of the world, its troubles and its challenges.

I want to encourage you not to let the prayer time pass. Where there is little prayer . . . little power. No prayer . . . no power. We have to pray. Is the devil in your house? He can't stay if you pray. Is the devil in your kids? He can't stay in there if you pray. Is the devil in you? He can't stay in you if you pray. There is no way for the wicked one and the Holy One to dwell in the same place. That's why the Lord encourages us to pray. That's why the devil does not want us to pray. When we pray, it is two-way communication with the Savior. We

31

should talk to God, but then we must stop and let God talk to us. I am not minimizing the praying that we do during church services, but we don't leave time for God to say anything—we only talk to God at the altar. Therefore, I say that Saturday evening would be a good time for us to talk to God, and then we can be silent and let God talk to us. This allows good and proper communication between God and us.

The writer of Luke tells us, *"And it came to pass in those days that he [Jesus] went out to the mountain to pray, and continued all night in prayer to God"* (Luke 6:12). Luke also told us, *"And it came to pass, as he was alone praying, his disciples were with him: and he asked them, saying, Whom say the people that I am?"* (Luke 9:18). As Jesus was in the process of praying, He received revelation. He found out information that could help prepare Him for the next leg of His ministry. Luke 9:28-29 says,

> *And it came to pass about an eight days after these sayings, he took Peter and John and James, and went up into a mountain to pray. And as he prayed, the fashion of his countenance was altered, and his raiment was white and glistering.*

Have you ever prayed long enough to be in the presence of God? Have you ever prayed long enough for your countenance and spirit to be altered? Have you ever prayed long enough that when you arose, you had a spiritual glow about you?

Our Tools: Faith

We have to have faith to be equipped, ready, qualified and prepared. God has created us and given us faith to help us have a relationship with Him. Hebrews 11:6 says: *"But without faith it is impossible to please him: for he that cometh to God must believe that he is, and that he is a rewarder of them that diligently seek him."* Concerning the circumstances you've been facing, you need to understand that it is not simply about what you are going through, but also that God is in the process of increasing your faith. He's trying to teach you to trust Him. The minute you say, "It is going to be all right," it gets all right—right then. But as long as you try to figure it out on your own––how not to go through it but go around it—then God says you have to go through situations in order to strengthen your faith and increase your belief in Him.

I feel as though I have wasted a lot of my spiritual life by saying, "God, don't let me go through anything now; just tell me what you want me to do and I will be obedient." Well, that worked fairly well until I needed additional power. Then it dawned on me: I had no experience, so I had no power. I didn't know how to fight any demons, because I hadn't fought any. God had made it easy for me. He'd been faithful to me. Then one day, I started having to fight some demons and I said, "God, do something!" He said, "No, you do something!" Has God ever told you to do something? I'm so thankful He told me to do something. That is what has given me the courage to carry out His plan for me to share the gospel of Jesus Christ with others, both near and far away.

Romans 1:17 tells us, *"For therein is the righteousness of God revealed from faith to faith: as it is written, The just shall live by faith."* The righteous shall live by faith. If you don't have faith, you can't live righteously. We have to have faith. Romans 10:17 adds, *"So then faith cometh by hearing, and hearing by the word of God."* Therefore, to increase faith we have to read, believe, and apply the Word. The only way to increase your faith is reading God's Word; and when that Word gets tested in you, then you will know that Word for yourself.

Without faith we can't reach the blessings and favors that God has prepared for us. We can't reach a better future. Everything that we deal with has no solution unless we have faith. I don't see everything that God is doing right now. Without faith, it is impossible to please God and to do the things that He is calling us to do. God wants us to keep moving at His appointed time, with the worthy tools He has given to us.

Chapter 4

Let Pain Work, Not Hurt

The goal of this chapter is to help us understand that our pain can have a positive affect for our lives. If you are in the midst of a painful situation, if you are going through the fire and challenges of life, you need to be reminded not just to let your pain hurt, but let your pain work!

Jesus spoke the words of Luke 23:34 at the time of His crucifixion—*"Then said Jesus, Father, forgive them; for they know not what they do. And they parted his raiment, and cast lots."*--and anyone who knows anything about crucifixion understands that it is the most cruel and gruesome type of death. Jesus died that type of death not because he had done something wrong, but rather because He loved us so much. Isn't it amazing to think that someone loves you so much that he or she would die for you?

When Jesus faced the crucifixion, He had been falsely accused by the religious leaders, He had been betrayed by those who were close to Him—He was denied by three of them--He had been beaten and rejected by His own people, and He had done nothing wrong. We can find ourselves in the message because most of us, when we go through pain, think we have done nothing wrong. Jesus was sinless, yet He went through all the pain of crucifixion anyway. When He was hanging on the cross, His words to the Father were "forgive them." While they were crucifying Him, He was praying for their forgiveness. What a great message for our hearts; we know that our pain does not have to just hurt, but we can also let it work!

We are challenged and encouraged to make sure that we are just as Jesus was. Christ in us, the hope of glory, means that we must let Christ manifest His life through us (see Colossians 1:27). We have to let Christ live through us, which means that we have to forgive people whether they deserve forgiveness in our minds or not. They deserve forgiveness because Jesus died for them. As you look at people, look at them not only in their circumstances but also as people for whom Jesus shed His blood. That is an awesome revelation for us to hold on to as we go through this life.

Pain and rejection will certainly come into our lives. No matter how we want to respond, God requires us to respond based upon our identity in Him. As Christians, we should not continue to behave like we did before we were saved. When we become Christians, it is necessary for us to change our behavior.

In order for pain to do more than just hurt, we need to learn to respond in a way that glorifies God. When we know that our life is designed to give God glory, we won't need to expend so much energy thinking about the painful situations are in our lives. So many times we get engrossed in how things are affecting us, when it is really not even about us. It is all about God wanting to do something in our lives and through our lives. If we just let Him, we will have the privilege of finding out that we can do more than we thought we could.

God Himself set up the opportunity for us to have a chance to keep moving forward. That very thing that you do not want to be bothered with is God's opportunity for you to move forward in a positive way. When we realize that God Himself set up the opportunity for us to be challenged and tested, we will yield to them, knowing they are designed for us to grow up in that area—to be strengthened in that area. The next time that a test comes up, we will have ammunition for it. We do not have to fall in the same trap again. We do not have to keep going through the same cycle. We can really stand up and receive our deliverance instead of dreading the challenge or test.

The Apostle Paul wrote in Galatians 4:4, saying, *"But when the fulness of the time was come, God sent forth his Son, made of a woman, made under the law."* God set it up. It was not Mary's work; but rather God's work. He set it up. Mary was just waiting for the manifestation of what she was promised. In the fullness of time, God brought

Christ forth, born of a woman and born under the law.

I am excited that God has me living in the perfect time for my life. Although it is the worst of times, it is also the best of times. When the world system is messed up, it is the time when the church can shine. There are opportunities everywhere. If you look, you can find an opportunity to bless someone's life.

Many, many years ago, the Hebrew Bible was established. The Jewish people had the law. The Greeks had an advanced language. The Romans had developed road systems so that the gospel could get out into the whole world. Jesus was born in a lowly manger with the animals so that He could identify with the common person and the common person could identify with Him. People who needed the Savior could also relate to the disciples, who were common men.

I often tell people I learned everything I know on the farm. I am a farm girl and I grew up on a farm in Greensboro, Alabama. I learned all the principles of sowing and reaping. I learned all the principles of a good work ethic right on the farm. When I moved to the city, all I had to do was implement everything I had already been taught. Most of the time, it is not about where you begin--it is where you are going with what you have. It is what you do with what you know that makes a difference. Many of us started in greater places than the farm and still have not accomplished much. If you take what you know and put it into practice, then God will give you more. If you are going to move forward in God, you will frequently experience pain.

Jesus came into the world to redeem us. It was a necessary transaction. The Father had established that no one could see Him and come to know Him in righteousness except by the shedding of blood. In order to fulfill the requirement of atoning for sin with the shedding of blood, Jesus had to come and shed His blood. If He had not shed His blood, we would still be slaughtering different kinds of animals for the remission of our sins. Aren't you glad Jesus came and took care of all that? There are some things that we do not think about that Jesus did for us, making life so much better.

Sometimes when we are on a journey, we experience unexpected detours and delays: a flat tire, the oil light comes on, bad weather, flight cancellations, etc. All kinds of things happen when you travel and it is to be expected. If you do not prepare for it, the delay is bound to happen. The more you prepare for a delay, the less likely you will experience one. Even if there is a slight delay, you will have given yourself ample time to make the necessary adjustments. We have to remember that both the journey of life and this journey as Christians has pitfalls. They both have unexpected situations that are going to come up. If you view yourself as someone who always requires pleasure and comfort, you are going to be frequently disappointed.

I love to be comfortable. I like the temperature just right. I like things clean and in order. I don't like a bunch of junk stuck in places. So to prove to myself that I was changing, my husband and I had children and grandchildren over during a certain holiday, and family members were everywhere at our house. I was glad they were there, so I was not complaining. We inflated every air mattress that we had. I was about to borrow some because I wanted everyone to have his or her own bed. My daughters said, "I can sleep with you, Mom!" I said, "No, you can't! Let's blow up another air mattress." If you have ever been to our home, you know there's a big common area. Well, it was full of air mattresses. There's a big dining room, and it was full of air mattresses. There's a library and it was full of air mattresses. At one point, I was putting an air mattress down in the hall. Not only did we inflate all of them, but we also left them all down during the holiday! I said to myself, "Girl, you're growing, you're changing!"

Last year, we would have had to let the air out of the mattresses, fold them up, put them away, pull them out again at night, and inflate them again. Don't tell me you can't change. You make up your mind to change and God will change you.

Furthermore, He will let you know whether you have changed or not.

During the entire holiday, the house was inundated with mattresses and all kinds of toys and I said, "Let's just leave it right there." The good news was I knew the holiday was temporary, before long everybody would be back where they belong, and I could clean up again! Just the mere fact that God gave me the grace, and it wasn't frustrating, was a blessing. Some of us live our lives so stressfully because we don't have the understating that we should just let go of some of this stuff that keeps us bound. It was good in its time and season, but you're in a new day!

The painful situations we will inevitably experience should do more than just hurt; they should also help us grow in grace. The Apostle James tells us that some pain and displeasure come from not getting what we want.

From whence come wars and fightings among you? come they not hence, even of your lusts that war in your members? Ye lust, and have not: ye kill, and desire to have, and cannot obtain: ye fight and war, yet ye have not, because ye ask not. Ye ask, and receive not, because ye ask amiss, that ye may consume it upon your lusts. (James 4:1-3)

First of all, if our titles of ourselves identify with satan's titles, they are going to sound like this: idiotic, selfish, ignorant, etc. When we use titles that identify with who satan thinks we are, we will have a difficult time believing that our pain can work for us.

Here's the good news! God has also given us titles! He has given us titles like conqueror, child of God, and beloved. All of the titles that God gives us require a different pain response. How we respond to the pain will have everything to do with the outcome.

Jesus Endured Pain for Our Benefit

Jesus knew that His suffering was crucial to His finishing the work that He was sent to the earth to do. When Peter tried to keep Jesus from being crucified, He called Peter satan (see Mark 8:31-33). Jesus was willing to keep moving to carry out His assignment even though He knew that it was going to be painful.

Jesus also identified with our pain, according to Hebrews 5:5 that says, *"So also Christ glorified not himself to be made an high priest; but he that said unto him, Thou art my Son, to day have I begotten thee."*

According to Isaiah 53:5, Jesus made it possible for us to be healed by His stripes. His suffering paid something for you. His suffering paid for your healing and your deliverance. He suffered so we do not have to suffer. There are some things we have to do, but we do not have to do what Jesus has already done for us. We can receive the healing that has already been paid for by Jesus.

The Apostle Paul tells us in Philippians 2:10 that someday, at the Name of Jesus, every knee will bow to Christ and every tongue will confess that He is Lord. Although He died a cruel death, He made it possible for us to know Him and receive Him as Lord. He doesn't have to worry about whether we accept Him or not, because the day will come when we will all know He is the Lord of lords and King of kings.

When Jesus died on the cross, it provided us an opportunity to be redeemed by His blood. We received an opportunity to gain direct access to the Father. In the same way, when we suffer, it provides opportunity for people to be reconciled. When you go through a trial or tribulation and then minister to people who are going through a similar situation, they can believe you—they can receive hope.

Everything we're going through is not about our suffering, it is so we can extend the same grace to someone else that was extended to us. We can comfort others the way we were comforted.

Blessed be God, even the Father of our Lord Jesus Christ, the Father of mercies, and the God of all comfort; Who comforteth us in all our tribulation, that we may be able to comfort them which are in any trouble, by the comfort wherewith we ourselves are comforted of God. (2 Corinthians 1:3-4)

We use the same comfort that we received to comfort other people. There are some things that I just wouldn't talk to some people about, either because I wouldn't trust what they would say or because they didn't have any experience in that area. Then there are some people who I would definitely trust because they have been through some things and know what they are talking about—people who would talk to me according to the Word and not just out of their experience. We are able to be comforted and receive confidence, especially if the person is walking in some kind of victory. Know that you have a right to decree and declare that victory. Jesus bought that victory for you!

When we go through circumstances and situations and we come through it giving God praise, honor and glory and stand up to the situation, then people around us get to see the glory of the Lord shine through our lives (see 1 Peter 4:12-14). So we say, "God show us your glory," but God can also show us His glory through someone else's life when they endure pain victoriously. God's glory will show through anyone's life when that person is living for Him.

A life that has not suffered is a life that will have no glory—a life that will have no reflection.

God shows through in the broken places of our lives. Can you think about the places where you consider yourself strong? We don't consult God in those areas, for we try to figure things out on our own. Here's the fact: there is no area of our lives that we "have it going on." None! We need Jesus when we wake up in the morning and we need to tell Him thank You! When we pop our eyes open so we can see, we ought to say thank You, Lord! When we get out of the bed and put our feet on the floor, we ought to say, "Thank You, Lord!" I'm just showing you how much you need Him. If you can stand up on your own, you ought to say "thank You!" We can't do anything without God. If you wake up and can think of one person who loves you, you ought to say "thank You Jesus."

Nothing Can Separate Us from God

As children of God, we can be confident that nothing can snatch us from the hand of God. So it doesn't matter what we go through, we should make up our minds that we will keep moving according to His plan for our lives. Furthermore, we should not allow other people to cause us to stop moving because of pain that we are experiencing. People can talk about your life and what it isn't, but people can't "unsave" you. Thanks be unto God that Romans 8:38-39 lets us know that no one can take us out of the hand of our Father.

For I am persuaded, that neither death, nor life, nor angels, nor principalities, nor powers, nor things present, nor things to come, Nor height, nor depth, nor any other creature, shall be able to separate us from the love of God, which is in Christ Jesus our Lord (Romans 8: 38-39).

Some people say that we can take ourselves out of the hand of God, but I disagree with that belief. If I could take myself out of God's hand, then it means that I would have to be in some other place. How can I be in another place and also be in God's hands? The still little voice in your heart is the Holy Spirit that seals us in God the day we are born again. If you've been born again, you've been sealed by the Holy Spirit in the body of Christ. Don't try to spend your life trying to get saved again; spend your life continuing to move in the things of God!

I realize that the more we keep moving for God, the less time we have to do things that are not important. We have more time to make a difference in the lives of other people

Oftentimes, when we experience pain, we withdraw from others and choose to go through our situation alone. Being alone can be dangerous and keeping challenges only in your mind can be even more dangerous, because that's where the enemy works—in our minds. That's why I talk about situations sometimes that may be uncomfortable for people, but it helps me to put the devil on Front Street and it helps me to be more accountable. So when people see me moving in a certain direction, they can help me stay the course.

The devil wants to rule over us in secrecy, especially when we are dealing with a painful situation. He wants to keep things quiet to make sure no one knows about what we are going through. If you make a decision to confess your challenges to someone else (as led by the Holy Spirit), they are able to keep you in prayer, and you are more likely to be in a better position to receive a breakthrough.

Pain hurts, but it doesn't have to just hurt. It can work for you and for others. Know that God is able to do something through your pain. He is able to cause you to work a great work for Him because of the pain you go through. Make sure you describe yourself according to the Word of God regardless of your painful situation.

Describe yourself with God's words. You are victorious, awesome, powerful, saved, sanctified, delivered, and healed. By your seeing the positive side of pain, know that you can also be a blessing to those who are going through a similar situation. They will see you walking in victory and be encouraged to do the same.

Chapter 5

Ability to Move Forward

We have all the power we need to keep moving. Sometimes, we think we come to church to get information—to get power—but what we really come to church for is to receive revelation from God. Without revelation, we really do not know and understand who we are. When we understand that by the grace of God, Christ in us, and the Holy Spirit in us, we have all the power we need to keep moving. Isn't that good news? We have all the power to do whatever it is that needs to be done. All we have to know is where to work and how to work it!

The main objective of this chapter is to encourage you to rely on the spiritual power God has provided and not on natural power—not on what we know and not on whom we know. Many times we help people, and then they want to be indebted to us because they think it is the right thing to do. However, I frequently remind people that whenever a person helps you, you should be thankful to God, for He is the one who told that person to help. Therefore, your being indebted is not unto a human being; it is still always unto the Lord.

It is important to keep this notion before us. If we don't, we get locked in by people and we end up indebting ourselves unnecessarily.

God has given us the power to keep moving. Power gives us the ability to move forward. There are two kinds of power: spiritual power and natural power. *Spiritual power is superior to natural powe*r and spiritual power should be received and never taken.

The Bible tells us about a boy in Mark 9 who was possessed with a demon spirit. The boy's father brought him to the disciples to have the spirit cast out, but they were not able to cast the spirit out. However, when the boy was brought to Jesus, He was able to cast the spirit out as recorded in Mark 9: 14-29:

> *And when he came to his disciples, he saw a great multitude about them, and the scribes questioning with them. And straightway all the people, when they beheld him, were greatly amazed, and running to him saluted him. And he asked the scribes, What question ye with them? And one of the multitude answered and said, Master, I have brought unto thee my son, which hath a dumb spirit; And wheresoever he taketh him, he teareth him: and he foameth, and*

gnasheth with his teeth, and pineth away: and I spake to thy disciples that they should cast him out; and they could not. He answereth him, and saith, O faithless generation, how long shall I be with you? how long shall I suffer you? bring him unto me. And they brought him unto him: and when he saw him, straightway the spirit tare him; and he fell on the ground, and wallowed foaming. And he asked his father, How long is it ago since this came unto him? And he said, Of a child. And ofttimes it hath cast him into the fire, and into the waters, to destroy him: but if thou canst do any thing, have compassion on us, and help us. Jesus said unto him, If thou canst believe, all things are possible to him that believeth. And straightway the father of the child cried out, and said with tears, Lord, I believe; help thou mine unbelief. When Jesus saw that the people came running together, he rebuked the foul spirit, saying unto him, Thou dumb and deaf spirit, I charge thee, come out of him, and enter no more into him. And the spirit cried, and rent him sore, and came out of him: and he was as one dead; insomuch that many said, He is dead. But Jesus took him by the hand, and lifted him up; and he arose. And when he was come into the house, his disciples asked him privately, Why could not we cast him out? And he said unto them, This kind can come forth by nothing, but by prayer and fasting. The disciples asked Jesus why they couldn't they cast the spirit out and Jesus replied, "This kind can come forth by nothing, but by prayer and fasting.

Mark 9:29 tells how we free ourselves from evil spirits to keep them from reigning in our lives. These spirits will only leave by fasting and praying. You cannot have just one; you must have both.

While in the process of taking back what the devil stole from us, the devil literally says, "Okay, I know you're going to take your stuff back. You got that revelation to get your stuff!" We are so excited when we get our stuff back. However, what we miss is that the devil has slipped in additional trouble for us when we take back the stuff he stole. His plan is to keep us distracted so we won't tell him to take back what he left with us. He gives us our stuff back, and then he backs up in an effort to make us believe that we do not have some of his mess. As long as he left something with us, he thinks he has some ownership of us. This is why proclamations and affirmations declaring God's Word will give us power to ensure there are no unsettled demonic claims against us.

We can tell the enemy to come and get his mess and take it back to the pit of hell where it belongs! Yes, you can take back what he stole from you and tell him he cannot leave his mess, such as fear, anxiety, stress, and troubles with you. These are not ours to claim! It is not our nature. It is not who we are. We shouldn't own it or claim it. This mess belongs to the devil, so we should tell him to take it back!

When Jesus came down from the mountain after His transfiguration, He noticed His disciples arguing because they could not cast out the demon from the boy who was possessed. After Jesus prayed a brief prayer, He delivered the boy from the demon. This is a critical message for ministers of the gospel. We can actually lose effectiveness when we say too much. We have the authority and power to say what needs to be said to the devil. Just tell the devil what he needs to do in the name of Jesus and be done.

The disciples were confused about why they could not cast out the devil from the little boy. The reason is that they did not have enough spiritual power. Have you ever been there? Have you tried to do a spiritual work and didn't have the spiritual power to do it? Yes, this kind of power only comes by fasting and praying. We have to spend that time seeking the power of God. We must ask God to give us more power. This mindset is asking God to fill us more with Him, more with His power and His presence. These are not just nice sounding clichés. They are absolutely necessary, because this world gets more wicked every day.

Yesterday's anointing is not sufficient for today. Today's anointing will not take care of tomorrow. That's why I get so excited about young people who take what they know and what adults know and put it all together in a season to receive victory. This has always been true! Even in our parents' generation, the same was true! It takes all of us to get it done. God is saying we can have the spiritual power we need. More often than not, we are trying to accomplish spiritual tasks with natural power, but it does not work. We must understand that natural and spiritual powers are always working.

Imagine this scenario: I am driving a vehicle and the engine doesn't have power. I am not going to get anywhere. I must have engine power to propel the car, and likewise, we must have spiritual power to do what God charges us to do. If we do not have spiritual power, we cannot move forward. We end up going in circles and accomplishing little. Our call is to make a difference and to get something done.

My message is to empower you so you can walk in victory, even outside of the church. I feel like I can trust the people I deal with in church, but I'm not saying that I have to let my guard down. However, I am thankful I live around people I can trust. Although I realize we have to be cautious in our interactions, I choose to trust first.

When you walk out of the church doors, the devil is waiting to challenge you. If he's not challenging you, you may be working on his team! If you are against the devil, he will be against you. If you are doing his kingdom damage, he will press you on every side.

One of the many ways the devil presses us is by discouraging us with a bad report. We must use our words to praise God no matter what kind of report we receive. I made up my mind a few years ago that I am just going to praise God no matter what's happening in my life.

People look at you when you are going through something, and they think you ought to look a certain way. When we don't react or respond in the usual way, it confuses people, and it also confuses the enemy. Instead of getting upset when you are going through something, choose to give God the praise and the glory and let Him determine how you will react.

We need the power of God to make sure we can get the work done. Acts 1:8 explains how God gave us power when He gave us the Holy Spirit. I know that when we get saved, the Holy Spirit begins to work in our lives. Nevertheless, I am a personal witness that we can be saved a long time and not be filled with the Holy Spirit. I was saved in a country church when I was not even twelve years old. When you get saved in the country, you really get saved. The saints will watch you and tell whether or not you need to go back to the altar, mainly because you have not changed a bit.

Nowadays, people get saved and do not think they have to change. They act the same way, do the same things, go to the same places, and have the same attitude. Yet, they say they are saved. As I mentioned, back in the day, the saints would take you back to the altar.

Although I was not even twelve years old when I got saved, I did not receive the Holy Spirit until I was twenty-seven years old. I knew I was saved. I was confident in my salvation because every sermon I heard was about getting saved. I was saved, but I had not heard about the Holy Spirit. I am one of those people who wants whatever God has for me. When you get the Holy Spirit, you get the power!

If you don't have the Holy Spirit, you don't have to be ashamed, but you ought to want to receive Him. Before I received the Holy Spirit, I was always asked by one of the ministers at our church, "Have you received the Holy Spirit yet?" I said, "I'm saved. Why are you asking me that?" She would just leave me alone for a time, but when I saw her again, she would ask, "Have you received the Holy Spirit yet?" I would say, "I'm saved. When I got Jesus, I got everything I needed." She said, "Yeah, but do you have the Holy Spirit?" She would ask me every time she crossed my path, but she didn't tell me how to get Him. I didn't know what to do, for her questions stirred something up in mea longing. Sometimes, all you need to do is ask a question and let the Holy Spirit take it from there.

Soon afterwards, somebody gave me a book that taught on how to become filled with the Holy Spirit. Thanks be unto God for the printed word.

I was driving down the expressway with that book on my dashboard one day. Every time I stopped while sitting in bumper-to-bumper traffic, I pulled out my book and read. All of a sudden, I got filled with the Holy Spirit. I was talking in tongues and celebrating with the Lord all the way to my destination. Something happened inside of me, and I could tell that it was something new that had happened. From that day until now, it has been consistent. I walk with God with so much more consistency. The Holy Spirit gives us power to walk in victory while on this earth. If you're not going to leave this earth right now, you're going to need the Holy Spirit. The Holy Spirit is the power of God. He is your help in the time of trouble. The Holy Spirit anoints you with power, and it is the anointing that breaks and destroys yokes of bondage. You need the Holy Spirit!

I used to get nervous when I empowered people to walk in the call of God over their lives, because you run the chance of their moving on to complete the work that God has given them. Sometimes, the work moves them away from the ministry. But every time I get a little nervous, the Holy Spirit comforts me by letting me know that I can ask God for what I want when people leave the ministry. So, every time someone answers their call, I say, "Lord, I would like twelve young people to replace that person." You know what God does? He does it! You will be amazed how God will honor your request. When you see the influx of young people, it's because I've asked God to give me twelve young people to replace people who left to answer the call on their lives.

Natural vs. Spiritual Power

Leaders must continue to give people the opportunity to develop, and that means that God has to give someone an ear to hear from the Spirit. Remember that there are two types of power—natural and spiritual.

All of us have some form of natural power. Some of us have a wonderful personality. While some people have a great personality, others are intelligent. When I'm not in the Spirit, I really don't have the greatest personality, but the anointing fills the void. I don't like the stage, but when I have to do it, the anointing makes the difference. God is able to make every grace abound to you to provide whatever you need according to what He has told you to do.

You can own your own weapon. That will give you some power! Some people have strong muscles, and some of us have pretty faces. Some people have natural power because they have money. When I talk about having money, I am talking about having enough money to make a difference and to help people who are in need. I thank God that I have money. I do help people and I'm thankful that I can.

There are others who know the right people. Knowing the right people can get you into some places, so there is power in knowing people. I am not minimizing our natural power.

In the story about the disciples not being able to cast the evil spirit out of the boy, Jesus demonstrated to His disciples His ability to do something they couldn't do. He let them know it was not natural power. What they needed was spiritual power, which was superior to natural power. When you need somebody to pray for you to be delivered, you need somebody with some spiritual power. The demon that possessed the boy had control over the boy. The boy's desire was to resist the demon in his physical strength, which wasn't much. Most of the time, when we're trying to overcome, we try to overcome in our physical strength and that just doesn't work.

When I call a fast at our ministry, some members participate and others do not. Even those who do still can't wait until the weekend gets here! We know how difficult it is to fast. We can go for a season, but before you know it, we end up binging!

After a while, willpower crashes and the binge happens. We just don't have that much willpower.

That's why fasting is a spiritual work. We have to ask the Holy Spirit to help us. You cannot just stop eating; you have to pray. It's not a weight loss plan, so whenever you fast and think it's a good opportunity to drop a few pounds, you can actually gain weight because your metabolism gets messed up.

Although the boy with the evil spirit desired to resist the demon in his physical strength, he was not able to do it. As a matter of fact, the demon forced the boy to do things he didn't want to do, like throwing himself in the fire and in the water.

If you are going through something, I dare you to fast and pray. Don't try to fast for fifty things. Go for one situation and fast and pray until it breaks. You know how you know when it's broken? When you fasted so long, you forgot being hungry. Now you know something is happening. I am talking about turning down your plate until God delivers you. He will do it! You don't have to keep the evil spirits that are vexing you. You have the power and it's spiritual.

Spiritual power can never be taken. You can only get it by receiving it from God. That's why most human beings end up falling short of having spiritual power— they try to take it. The stuff we can take we will manipulate, take from someone, use the Scriptures, etc. There are some people with silver tongues, but I'm not one of them. There are people who can talk you right out of things you know you shouldn't be giving up or talk you into getting stuff that you know you shouldn't be getting. We have to remember that this spiritual power will help us not to be deceived when people try to manipulate us—even when we're doing stuff we don't even want to be doing.

We can only receive this power when God gives it to us. It has to be authentic. You can't manufacture it. You can't pretend because the devil will look at you and say, "Jesus I know, but who are you?" Spiritual power comes from spending time in His presence. This is not about the spectacular. If we live from one miracle to the next, then we will need a miracle every day and we will be living from one crisis to the other. I don't want to live from crisis to crisis. I just want to walk with God. The Christian walk is a walk with God. We can walk in victory every day, not just waiting for the next miracle to happen.

Everyone needs supernatural spiritual power. It's received from God into a life that is surrendered to Him. If we don't surrender to God, we will not get power from God. This awareness comes from knowing that if God doesn't do it, it's not going to get done. If He doesn't do it in us, it will never happen. We cannot take anything from God. We must receive from Him. He will give power to us when He knows that we are ready to receive it for His glory! The only reason God gives us His supernatural power is when He knows we're going to use it for His glory. He knows us, and He knows what we're going to do. I like to think I know myself, but I believe God knows me better in that He knew me before I was formed in my mother's womb. When He says, "No" or says, "Wait" to me, I believe He knows best. I believe He knows that if I got this or accomplished that, I would not give Him glory. It would puff me up and get me off track. That's why I say, *"Thank You, Lord, for not letting me go that way."*

Spiritual power comes from the Holy Spirit, and it comes for a very specific and unique purpose. That is so we might live for God and do His bidding. Matthew 10:1 states, *"And when he had called unto him his twelve disciples, he gave them power against unclean spirits, to cast them out, and to heal all manner of sickness and all manner of disease."* Jesus gave His disciples authority over evil spirits. Why? Not for them to boast, and not for them to hang out a sign that says, "I do deliverance!" We don't do deliverance. When deliverance happens, God does it! God needs a vessel and He wants to use you, but He wants the glory to go back to Him.

Matthew 10:19-20 states, *"But when they deliver you up, take no thought how or what ye shall speak: for it shall be given you in that same hour what ye shall speak. For it is not ye that speak, but the Spirit of your Father which speaketh in you.*" The Word clearly states He also gave them the Holy Spirit so He could tell them what to say when they were attacked. We need to rely on the Holy Spirit a whole lot more in our business dealings, because too many times we are doing business without the Holy Spirit. We are leaning on our own power. Our own power can deceive us because we only know so much, but when we have the Holy Spirit, we have heaven and the whole heavenly hosts. Do you know you have ministering spirits assigned to you? They only work through your spiritual power, not through your natural power. They are there to tell you, "No, don't sign that yet." Even though it sounded like the right thing.

You've been asking God to make this thing happen, and all of a sudden, you have the opportunity to sign a contract. The Lord is saying with just a little nudge, "Don't sign it. Wait twenty-four hours." And in those twenty-four hours, all hell breaks loose and you say, "Thank God I didn't do that." Don't always think when there's a "No" that you are missing something. Sometimes, when there's a "No," you're being protected from something.

There are a whole lot of things that God has protected me from. When I look back over my life, I realize that it was God who was protecting me. I'm not saying I was not kicking and screaming, calling the saints to pray. I did everything I knew to do, but God said, "No." Then after a while, I said, "Lord, thank You. You saw what I couldn't see!"

When the church in Antioch wanted to send out workers, the Bible tells us:, *"As they ministered to the Lord, and fasted, the Holy Ghost said, Separate me Barnabas and Saul for the work whereunto I have called them"* (Acts 13:2). The Lord used the Holy Spirit to set apart Paul and Barnabas for the work of the ministry that He called them to. The Holy Spirit guided them through that process. The spiritual power of God is always at work. God does not empower us to be rich or famous or in control, although this can happen in our obedience.

But the empowerment is for us to obey God, to give Him praise and to see that everything that we have brings glory to His name. In that process, many of us will be rich and powerful. But you can't start out with being rich and powerful as your goal. Your goal has to be to give glory to God. In that journey, you might find that all of a sudden you're rich, famous, and powerful--and whatever else God wants to give you--but that cannot be your driving force.

We need to surrender to God today. We need to admit that we need the power of God. We need to admit that we may all have a measure of natural power that we're very proud of having.

Today say, "Yes" to the Lord and give up all of your control. That can be hard, but we have to do it. How do we give it up? We must admit we need help to get things done. We tell the Lord, "I give You my control today." You start in your mind by making the decision. When you feel yourself wanting to take charge and take over and control the situation again, remind yourself, *that's not my battle anymore; it's the Lord's.* We need to use every resource that we have to step into that place of submission. When this is all said and done, it will be God who gives us that victory.

As I understood this process, God said, "Listen, stretch outside of your comfort zone because what you need is on the other side. You must let this happen because, when you get through with it, it will benefit the body of Christ." You are never going to trust God unless you do something different from what you did the last time.

Surrender everything to God. You must allow the Holy Spirit to get into position to power up your life like it's never been powered before. That power will be expressed through you as God works in your life--you can keep moving through the power of God!

Chapter 6

Desire to Complete the Work

Jesus states in John 14:12, *"Verily, verily, I say unto you, He that believeth on me, the works that I do shall he do also; and greater works than these shall he do; because I go unto my Father."* We must have a desire to complete the works that Christ has already promised we will do. Desire creates a since of passion.

God has prepared us so that we have everything in us we need to serve Him and to do what He has called us to do, both individually and collectively—we have the time, talent, testimony, and resources. God always provides us with the tools we need. He asks us to use what we have, start where we are, and do what we can. As we follow His plan for our lives, we receive increase. Passion is a required part in order to do what God expects us to do. Most people need to be motivated to stay faithful. We have to stay faithful until we hear the Father say, as written in Matthew 25:21, *"Well done thy good and faithful servant."* We may not stay faithful in all matters. Nevertheless, we ought to stay faithful to God's work and His Word. This should be our goal.

Many times people try to think and talk as if there is going to be additional time after this life, yet the work that we do in this life will not be continued in the next life. No matter what we will be doing in the next dispensation, it won't be the same as what we are doing now. For example, our timing is attached to the dash—the beginning of our life and the end of our natural life. Remember, this is the appointed time to keep moving to carry out God's plan for your life.

If you are responsible for a task at church in an area in which you have not operated, you need to know how to complete the task. One of the main things the church needs to do is train, equip, and qualify people for doing ministry. We qualify participants for all kinds of responsibilities for business success. However, the Christian mandate is qualifying people for the gospel ministry.

If you're in a congregation or business and leaders are expecting you to do something and you don't know how to do it, shame on them. They should ensure that the vision, the work, and the how to accomplish the task are clear.

Christ Completed His Assignment

We need to thank God that Jesus had the desire to complete what He started. Can you just think for a moment where we would be if Jesus had not had the desire to finish what He started? You do know that He could have stepped down from the cross. However, the decision He made to stay on the cross was not because He needed to be there, but because we needed Him to be there. On that cross, He stayed and died for our sins so that we could have the right to everlasting life.

One of the main things about the crucifixion story is in John 19:30 when Jesus said, *"It is finished."* In other words, He was born of a virgin named Mary, He lived and prepared Himself at twelve years of age to do the work of His Father, and it is then at around the age of thirty that He reappears on the scene. It is at this time that He says, *"It is finished."* In other words, His message was an indication that He had completed the work that God called Him to do. If God calls your name today, would you be able to say that you are on course and have finished what He placed in your heart and hands to do? Or would you have to say, "Lord, give me something else to do." Or would you have to ask, "Lord, can you give me another minute as I still have some business I need to take care of."

When Jesus hung on the cross with blood running down His body, He experienced pain and gruesomeness as He died for us. His experience on the cross was one of, if not the most excruciating trial that anyone has ever faced. He was beaten, battered, and bruised until flesh literally fell from His body. We should all pause and reflect on how Jesus suffered and died so that we might have life.

It was an inhumane trauma for Him to go through, yet He did it just for us. What a mighty God we have and should serve who gave His all for us!

When we understand the significance of the events from the cross, we realize the critical role of having passion for our spiritual responsibilities. Additionally, remembering the suffering of Christ on the cross places passion into the message of the gospel. When we don't understand the price that has been paid for our salvation, we take this sacrifice for granted. This is because we are unable to comprehend and appreciate the importance of this sacrifice and our subsequent salvation.

When we receive a revelation of what Jesus really did for us, we will surely have passion come into our hearts, minds, and souls. I believe one of the things that has happened to the Church is that we've gotten into preaching such a "good news" message that we have left out the spiritual significance of the cross. There has to be hope in the Christian message. I ardently believe we have to make sure that the lessons from the cross serve as the cornerstone of the gospel message.

Consider if you will that without the lessons from the cross, there is neither power nor passion in the gospel message. Instead, without the relevance of the cross, the spiritual message is devoid of power. As noted in the preceding paragraphs, the passion and the cross are integrated and extend the urgency and timeliness of the message. Note that

Jesus said He had come to do what God had sent Him to do. Now, it is our job—our spiritual legacy—to continue and extend where possible this work, which has yet to be completed. It requires all of us to have a desire to get it done.

Without the cross, there is no power in the gospel message. Without the cross, there is only a positive affirmation. The gospel is only positive thinking. It is only a positive communication, and it is devoid of power to change lives without the cross. The cross is what put passion in the Word. The lessons from the cross put the intense feelings and emotions in the communication. The cross is what put the urgency in this gospel message. Remember when the disciples were running scared? Jesus' critics were mocking Him, and He said, "It is okay what they say about me because it's finished. I'm leaving you here to do what you're supposed to do, but as for My work here on earth, I'm finished--I have done what I came to do."

He did everything His Father called Him to do, letting nothing go His own way, but everything going according to what His Father had asked of Him. Remember, He had just cried out a few hours before, saying, *"Lord, why have You forsaken Me?"* (Matthew 27:46).

So it wasn't that He was feeling good about this situation. He was in a state of desperate passion. He was in desperate grief about the situation. He first asked His Father, "Why have You forsaken Me, " and then he said in obedience, "It is finished."

Transforming Our Desire into Action

In the process of developing a desire to complete the work that you have been assigned, sometimes you may feel forsaken. It doesn't mean you need to quit. You may also feel as if you cannot keep moving forward because you do not know what you're going to do next. This is still not a good reason to give up. Simply stay the course and do that which you believe God has told you to do. Maintain strong prayers, strong belief, fortify your God-given desires, and He will see you through all manner of challenges.

Even though Jesus might have felt alone and abandoned (at times) by the Father, He refused to give in; and He kept His courage and faith in His Father. Many times, we, too, feel alone and that no one cares or is listening to our cries. Nevertheless, stay the course and do not give up!

If you're going to keep moving forward in God, you must have the desire to see it through no matter what. There will be plenty of opportunities to quit; but I promise you, you have to make up your mind that you won't quit no matter what.

From the moment that you begin a journey and get into the vehicle, you won't get there if you don't have 100 percent commitment to get where you want to go. For example, when I get up in the morning to go to church, I get in the car and then Dr. Holmes starts the engine. If we had not been 100 percent committed to traveling to the church, we might have turned the engine off and gone back into the house.

By the way, there are some Sundays when I feel like doing just that. Also, there are some Sundays that I wake up at 5:30 a.m., hit the alarm button on the clock, and I say to myself, *Let me just turn off the clock and wake up when I wake up.*

However, due to the level of desire to fulfill my responsibility and the calling on my life, I still get up and begin to do that which I am called to do. Still, there's something that nudges me and says, "You know you can't lie back down—get up because people are expecting you. You can't quit. You can't stop right here. This is not the day for you not to show up. This is not the day for you to be late for church. You have to get up now because if you don't get up now, you won't arrive on time."

So again, you have to be 100 percent committed to your calling—your responsibility and your spiritual mission—or you won't show up.

Keeping the Faith

When we establish a relationship with God, we make a commitment to be faithful as a believer at every opportunity. On a daily basis we face trials and tribulations (such as divorce, illness, or death of a loved one), yet in spite of these realities, we must stay the course and do that which God calls us to do. Yes, all manner of tragedies happen; but in spite of these events, we must stay on course and carry out our work.

Our ability to obey God should not be contingent upon how smoothly our lives run, and I thank God for this fact. If smoothly-running lives were the factor, many of us would have good reason and the right to quit. However, Jesus has shown us that in spite of personal pain and agony, we can and must finish what He started. We face great challenges, and some of these events alone would give us a reason to quit. Yet Jesus has shown us that in spite of the personal pain and agony we face, we can and must continue to go forth with commitment to complete our God-given desires.

This Is Not the Time to Take a Break

Remember, for every stoplight we reach and for every person we meet along the way, it's important to the journey that we complete our task. If we quit or take a break from being obedient to God—*Lord knows I've tried to do this*—we will discover that, sad to say, it does not work. If and when we quit, we cheat ourselves out of the opportunity to do something great for God. Another thing about quitting is that every time we quit and have to start over again, we lose precious ground. Yes, God is gracious, and yes, we can have a fresh start; but when we quit, we miss opportunities to witness and be a blessing to others who may not know who Jesus is. I love that God is about second chances, because if it were not for that, we would truly become hopeless cases. Keep in mind that when we quit, it costs us greatly. I want to encourage you to make up your mind not to quit and to stay focused on what God has called you to do.

By definition, desire is a strong feeling of wanting to have something or wishing for something to happen. As you will recall (and reflect on), Jesus exemplified the greatest example of how desire works in ministry. He demonstrated this through His being prepared for whatever came His way. We see evidence of His being prepared whenever Jesus was called upon to make sure all had heard and had understood the message and deeds that He delivered and set forth.

Additionally, Jesus employed a direct purpose for those lessons that He taught and the miracles that He brought forth. In these moments, He showed an intensity and fervor so that the flock would remember His work and mission. He also accepted pain in such a way as to teach humility as well as spiritual stamina. His life story also shows how He held great power and might, yet He honored God by all that He did. Finally, His obedience shows us the importance of having a desire and passion to complete the work that we must do.

We are not inherently good within ourselves. Instead, it is God who gives us this goodness and grace and teaches us that we can do all things through Him who strengthens us. (Philippians 4:13 says, *"I can do all things through Christ which strengtheneth me."*) All the way to the cross, Jesus trusted the preparation that God had made in Him to make it all the way up Calvary's hill. He also kept His faith in His Father, our God, to take care of Him and to carry out God's promise to us. So, He accepted and bore the rugged cross in order that we could enjoy the right to life and forgiveness.

Jesus trusted the Word of God even though He knew that quoting it would make the religious leaders angry. Mathew 26:64 states, *"Jesus saith unto him, Thou hast said: nevertheless I say unto you, Hereafter shall ye see the Son of man sitting on the right hand of power, and coming in the clouds of heaven."*

When He started to talk about who He was, they said He was blaspheming; yet He said it anyway! We have to say it anyway as well. Let's repeat this powerful message--"You have to say it anyway!" You have to do it anyway. It doesn't matter if what you say bothers others, you must continue to obey and follow God. Jesus relied on prayer for strength when He faced adversities even until His death. Luke 22:39 states, *"And he came out, and went, as he was wont, to the mount of Olives; and his disciples also followed him."*

An example of one of His challenges was when He was in the Garden of Gethsemane praying with His disciples, and the Bible says sweat was pouring from Him like blood. Yet, He continued to pray. This shows how He trusted that the circumstances would fulfill all righteousness even though it was painful. Consequently, this may happen to us when we feel great passion about important matters of the Spirit. It requires pain, sacrifice, and strong belief to go forward and complete the work for the Kingdom. It requires agony and commitment. It does cost us something. Luke 22:47 highlights the betrayal that Jesus experienced: *"And while he yet spake, behold a multitude, and he that was called Judas, one of the twelve, went before them, and drew near unto Jesus to kiss him."*

Desire to Fulfill Your Purpose

By the way, fulfilling your purpose causes you to love your enemies, even if they are in the process of attacking you. You must first make a decision to love and forgive your enemies. In Luke 23:34, Jesus says, *"Forgive them for they don't know what they're doing."* Interestingly, the more I walk this Christian journey, the more I find myself using this message that Jesus spoke. The key is if you try to explain to people about forgiving others when they do you wrong, they may not accept it because it sounds self-serving. However, we know these powerful, healing and redemptive words from

Jesus are an example to us as members of the Church of the Living God.

For me, this message from Jesus has been an opportunity to grow and gain favor and credibility. I am grateful to God that I reached this new place in my spiritual walk and embraced it. Conversely, I hesitate to say too loudly that I have learned to forgive because every time I say this, I get another test from God! Now, I find myself less annoyed when people cross my path, because I can take a deep breath, exhale, and allow the Spirit of God to guide and temper my feelings. Jesus' most loving act toward His enemies was to humbly offer Himself as a ransom for their sins.

Think about the scenario: The crowd is crucifying Jesus, yet He is dying for their sins. This is the greatest example of true and unwavering passion. That's why we should never commit evil for evil. We cannot choose to treat people like they treat us and remain Christian and true to the admonitions of God. We must remain faithful, consistent and called to the purpose and work that God has assigned us to do.

Desire for Missions and Outreach

It's nerve-racking and highly disappointing sometimes when you train people and they don't stay and work the Word. However, that's not our issue to ponder and waste valuable time on! Instead, our focus is to always do the call that God has placed on us, and this is to train people for work in the local, national, and international spiritual arenas. People come in these doors, and I say, "Come on in and get to work so I can pour in you all that I can pour in you, and you can pour in here what you have to share with us. My job is to make sure I'm fulfilling my mission while you are here—to train you."

I believe God is faithful in that there will always be those who are willing to get the work done. These things should encourage you to want to protect yourself from burnout and overwork. It is important for the senior leaders to take care of themselves.

For example, as a Senior Pastor, I assign five or more people on the podium to share the workload so that they can receive on-the-job training. We have all seen the ministries where you know exactly who is going to read the Scriptures, lead the prayers, deliver the sermons and say everything else that's going to be said every Sunday, every Wednesday, and any other day when services are planned.

At our ministry, you may not know who will be on the program or which leader will deliver the sermon for the day. Our church is a training church that prepares and sends out new, trained, capable, and committed leaders to extend the work and the Word of God. We are committed to the founding vision and church mandate.

Desire Will Cause You to Love Others

Jesus washed the feet of and shared a meal with Judas, who betrayed him. In John 13, as the crowd screamed, *"Crucify Him,"* He answered not a word but allowed the fatal betrayal and rejection to continue. Mark 15:13 states, *"And they cried out again, Crucify him."* Jesus prayed for forgiveness for those who were crucifying Him as recorded in Luke 23:34, *"Then said Jesus, Father, forgive them; for they know not what they do."*

There will be times when you simply do not feel like loving someone, but love for our Savior will let you turn your back on the situation and your face to the person. I believe God is calling us to a new level of accountability, because the people He's going to send to us are not going to be accustomed to church rituals and procedures. Instead, they will arrive from all walks of life. Perhaps they will not know when to raise their hands or stand up at the appropriate times or understand other church standards and practices. Therefore, what are you going to do, or how should this lack of understanding be handled? You have to allow God to work it out in the hearts of the people, and thereby, let the training flow in a comfortable and spiritually safe manner.

When you desire the things of God, sometimes you will endure pain. You see it coming. You know it's going to be painful. But instead of trying to protect your heart from it, you lean into it.

You say to yourself, *"Okay, this is how it's going to be. Therefore, let me just embrace this moment."* Progress cannot begin until you accept and embrace the moment. As long as you stand in resistance, you cannot expect progress and it will not occur. It only happens when you say "Yes" to our Father. Then He joins in with us, and the outcome becomes His responsibility. Jesus repeatedly told His disciples that He would be betrayed, beaten, and crucified, yet He kept moving forward in God's plan. Think about this: He knew what was going to happen, but it didn't stop Him from doing the will of His Father.

A defining experience from my past that held me back for so many years is that I was a leader from childhood within my family system. I allowed my siblings to think I knew what I was doing. If they didn't agree with me, I became angry with them, so they let me tell them what to do. I really didn't want to lead. I didn't want the responsibility of leading. When I did lead, however, I selfishly wanted to lead the way I desired. Guess what happened? God didn't put me in a situation where I had to accept another's leadership role. Instead, He gave me an entire family to lead, and then worldwide opportunities to lead. What can I say other than, "But God!" Subsequently, one day I entered the pulpit saying, "I'm enjoying preaching today!" I also said to myself, *What is happening and who was this woman talking?* But God! God works it out in your life because of the desire, the passion, the commitment, and the fulfillment of your holy purpose in His name and according to His glory for your life of service to Him.

Desire and passion are so committed to the purpose of God's power that they will drive you to be subjected to it before you are an instrument of the power. In other words, you'll be obedient and subservient to the purpose before you have the power to do it. You will become accountable to the purpose even before you have the power to get the job done. The reason so many of us don't do some things we should do is because we don't want to become embarrassed and look foolish in the eyes of others. We want it to appear as if we know what we're doing. Specifically, men don't like to be embarrassed. They don't want to appear as if they do not know what they're doing. They want to know what is expected of them well before they get started, and they desire detailed explanations when you share information or make a request of them.

Even if they mess up, we must simply allow them to make their own mistakes; and by all means do not—I repeat, do not—correct them. Men don't want to look foolish and out of touch! My purpose for this reference to men and their peculiarities is that I want to help us all to understand that men think differently than women; and because of that, they are a little bit slower to get engaged.

There's a real simple reason men don't get engaged as quickly, and I thank God for giving me revelation and understanding of why that is. It's not that they don't want to; they just want to understand clearly their roles and responsibilities. Don't tell them when they mess up. Just leave them alone and pray that God will reveal their discrepancies to them. And if He doesn't shed this light, then you just smile! Those of you who have been trying to get men to get engaged, make sure you explain everything thoroughly and clearly and give them room to do it their way. I like to say get the gift and forget about the personality!

God's Power Will Help You

We have to apply God's power to resist reacting in anger. None of us are without the capability for getting angry. If anyone says he does not get angry, he is just basically lying. As human beings, we all become angry at times, but we all respond differently. If I get angry in the natural, you will know it. But there are other people who can get angry with you and they just sulk, shut down, and get their feelings hurt. It's important that we make sure we pray to let God's power help us not to react inappropriately. Jesus could have easily resisted the arrest of the soldiers. He was mocked, and He was beaten, and He could have resisted the arrest; but because of passion, He chose not to as it is written in Luke 22:63: "*And the men that held Jesus mocked him, and smote him.*" He was mocked by the soldiers who challenged Him to save Himself (which He could have done, by the way), but He voluntarily allowed every evil thing to be done to Him. (As He said to His disciples in the Garden of Gethsemane, *"Thinkest thou that I cannot now pray to my Father, and he shall presently give me more than twelve legions of angels?"* (Matthew 26:53).

Jesus could have easily come off the cross if He had wanted to do so. By staying on the cross, He voluntarily used the power God had given Him to endure the pain and agony. There are many of us who are in some pressing situations and thinking about quitting. But I'm here to challenge you to take quitting out of your thoughts. Don't allow quitting to be an option.

Sister Bradley, who is a Deaconess at our ministry, said something in a women's meeting that really spoke to me. She said, "There are some things worth fighting for, and there are some things you have to get your fists ready to strike as well!" It just depends on what it is, but don't quit so quickly. You have to do the work, finish the job, and allow your strength—your passion—to have its way in your life.

The God-given desires within us strive each day to hear the Father say, "Well done, thy good and faithful servant." Every day--not just once in a while, but daily--we must walk with God and trust Him in all things. Matthew 25:23 states, *"His lord said unto him, Well done, good and faithful servant; thou hast been faithful over a few things, I will make thee ruler over many things: enter thou into the joy of thy lord.*" If we don't walk daily with God, we cannot walk with Him at all. Think on this concept: We don't get a moment off from walking with God. Every time we stop walking with God, even for a minute, we lose valuable ground. That's why we have to be determined to stay the course, which means that we do not change and do not shift.

The only way Jesus could announce that it was finished was because He knew that the goal and mission God had given Him to fulfill had been done. The only way we're going to be able to say, "It's finished" is to know what God said and go about doing this work. Make sure we don't spend unnecessary time trying to hear other people say, "Well done." Have that peace in your heart from knowing this is the will of God concerning you. Why? Because if there were five people and you told something to the group of five, each one of them would probably have different opinions. So who's right? It doesn't matter! All that matters is what God said and that you obey Him.

As Elder Hayes, who is a member of our church, says, "If it was God in the beginning, it will be God in the end, and if it wasn't God in the beginning, you can't make it God in the ending. And in a minute, everybody will know if it was God or not." Stay the course. When you don't finish God's business, you will have left an unmet need in somebody's life. This is not a casual situation.

Someone is counting on you, and there is an only then will you hear the Father say, "Well done, because you accepted the call to do something now." As it is written in Matthew 25:21: *"His lord said unto him, Well done, thou good and faithful servant: thou hast been faithful over a few things, I will make thee ruler over many things: enter thou into the joy of thy lord."*

The end of the story is that God has prepared you and empowered you to keep moving. He wants you to continue the work He started. Paul said in Philippians 3:12: *"I press on that I may lay hold on that for which Christ Jesus has already laid hold on for me."* (NKJV) He's already gotten power for us all, and all we have to do is do our part—to get up and get going in the direction that God has told us to go. We must . . . Keep Moving!

About the Author

Bishop Ruth W. Smith Holmes serves as Senior Pastor of Light of the World Christian Tabernacle International, headquartered in Stockbridge, Georgia. In 1982 she married the founder of Light of the World Christian Tabernacle International Inc, the Late Archbishop Jimmie Lee Smith.

Bishop Ruth was consecrated as Archbishop in 2009 and became the first female consecrated to the office of Bishop over an International Association or Diocese Worldwide. She also serves as Archbishop of Light of The World Christian Tabernacle International Association which has ministries in 13 countries with a membership over 200,000.

Bishop Ruth holds a Master's in Biblical Counseling and Doctorate in Ministry from Biblical Life College and Seminary in Marshfield, Missouri. In 2008 she became a published author of a book entitled "A Word on Love."

In 2010 Bishop Ruth married Dr. Rickie Holmes, who has joined the efforts of The Light leadership to fulfill the vision. They share six children and ten grandchildren who fully support the ministry. The legacy of love continues.

Contact Information

Booking

Light of the World Christian Ministries
5883 Highway 155 North
Stockbridge, GA 30281
678.565.7001
lotwct@comeintothelight.org
www.comeintothelight.org

Purchasing

678.565.7001
www.comeintothelight.org

Publisher Information

MEWE, LLC
404.482.3135
mewecorporation@gmail.com
www.mewellc.com